PROFESSIONAL CHEERLEADING

Leah Kaminski

AV² provides enriched content that supplements and complements this book. Weigl's AV² books strive to create inspired learning and engage young minds in a total learning experience.

Your AV² Media Enhanced books come alive with...

Audio
Listen to sections of the book read aloud.

Key Words
Study vocabulary, and complete a matching word activity.

Video
Watch informative video clips.

Quizzes
Test your knowledge.

Embedded Weblinks
Gain additional information for research.

Slideshow
View images and captions, and prepare a presentation.

Try This!
Complete activities and hands-on experiments.

... and much, much more!

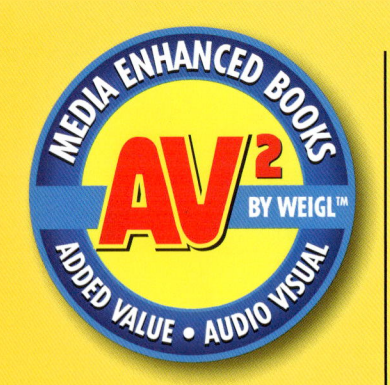

Go to www.av2books.com, and enter this book's unique code.

BOOK CODE

AVV92536

AV² by Weigl brings you media enhanced books that support active learning.

Published by AV² by Weigl
350 5th Avenue, 59th Floor
New York, NY 10118
Website: www.av2books.com

Copyright © 2020 AV² by Weigl
All rights reserved. No part of this publication may be reproduced, stored in a retrieval system, or transmitted in any form or by any means, electronic, mechanical, photocopying, recording, or otherwise, without the prior written permission of the publisher.

Library of Congress Cataloging-in-Publication Data
Names: Kaminski, Leah, author.
Title: Professional cheerleading / Leah Kaminski.
Description: New York, NY : Weigl, [2020] | Series: Cheerleading | Includes index. | Audience: K to Grade 3.
Identifiers: LCCN 2019012098 (print) | LCCN 2019016813 (ebook) | ISBN 9781791109967 (Multi User ebook) | ISBN 9781791109974 (Single User ebook) | ISBN 9781791109943 (hardcover : alk. paper) | ISBN 9781791109950 (softcover : alk. paper)
Subjects: LCSH: Cheerleading--Vocational guidance--Juvenile literature. | Cheerleading--Equipment and supplies--Juvenile literature. | Cheerleaders--Juvenile literature.
Classification: LCC LB3635 (ebook) | LCC LB3635 .K363 2020 (print) | DDC 791.6/4--dc23
LC record available at https://lccn.loc.gov/2019012098

Printed in Guangzhou, China
1 2 3 4 5 6 7 8 9 0   23 22 21 20 19

052019
103118

Project Coordinator: Heather Kissock
Designer: Ana Maria Vidal

Every reasonable effort has been made to trace ownership and to obtain permission to reprint copyright material. The publishers would be pleased to have any errors or omissions brought to their attention so that they may be corrected in subsequent printings.

Weigl acknowledges Getty Images, Shutterstock, and Alamy as its primary image suppliers for this title.

PROFESSIONAL CHEERLEADING

Contents

AV² Book Code 2

The World of Professional Cheerleading 4

History of Professional Cheerleading 6

Professional Cheerleading Timeline 8

How Professional Cheerleading Works .. 11

Athletes and Coaches 12

The Right Tools 14

The Right Moves 16

Getting Involved 18

Profile: Regina Bailey 20

Quiz 22

Key Words/Index 23

Log on to www.av2books.com 24

The World of Professional Cheerleading

Professional cheerleaders perform for thousands of fans. They wear sparkling outfits. They cheer for football and basketball teams. Professional cheerleading is different from other types of cheer. Dance skills are very important.

The Raiderettes have 31 members. They cheer for the Oakland Raiders football team in Oakland, California.

Professionals do not only cheer at sports games. They often go to **charity** events. Many are on television shows. These cheerleaders carry themselves well. They are also well-spoken.

Professionals learn how to be leaders. They build friendships with team members. Many keep these friendships for life. They reunite at special events. One of these events is the National Football Cheerleaders **Alumni** Reunion. It is held every two years.

Only **16 cheerleaders** make the Dallas Cowboy Cheerleaders' show group. The group travels and performs around the world.

About **80 percent** of National Football League (NFL) teams have cheerleaders.

Professional Cheerleading 5

The Dallas Cowboys Cheerleaders were first on television in 1978. They were in a show called the *NBC Rock-n-Roll Sports Classic*.

History of Professional Cheerleading

The Baltimore Colts were the first pro sports team to have a cheerleading **squad**. The squad formed in the 1950s. At that time, cheerleaders wore baggy sweaters and ponytails. They performed traditional cheers. In 1970, Tex Schramm was the general manager for the Dallas Cowboys. He created professional cheerleading as it is known today. Schramm started the Dallas Cowboys Cheerleaders (DCC). In 1972, he turned the squad's cheerleaders into dancers. The DCC became very famous.

In 1983, North Carolina State University cheerleaders cheered their team to the top spot in college basketball.

STUNT TEAM

The Baltimore Ravens are the only NFL team with a **coeducational** cheerleading **stunt** team. There are 21 men on the squad. A stunt team is different from a **sideline** cheerleading team. The men hold and twist their female team members. They throw them high in the air in complicated formations.

Other teams soon tried to copy the DCC's success. They became more dance-based. They changed their uniforms. Tryouts became more competitive. By the 1980s, almost every NFL and National Basketball Association (NBA) team had dance teams. The newest NFL dance team is the New York Jets' Flight Team. It was formed in 2007.

Professional Cheerleading

Professional Cheerleading Timeline

From the type of routines to who can join a dance team, much has changed since the beginning of professional cheerleading.

The DCC's uniforms have had six changes since 1972.

8 Cheerleading

1954 The Baltimore Colts NFL team is the first professional team to have cheerleaders. The cheerleaders are Colts fans. They cheer with the team's marching band.

1976 NFL cheerleaders are seen across the country for the first time. The DCC perform at Super Bowl X. The Indiana Pacemates form. This is the first professional NBA cheer team.

1978 Dance teams are inspired by the DCC. Squads make many changes. Uniforms, routines, and tryouts change. Every squad wants more **publicity**. *Sports Illustrated* magazine calls 1978 the "Great Cheerleading War of 1978."

1997 The DCC win the first **USO** Spirit of Hope award. From 1979 to 2018, the DCC perform on 83 USO tours. This is more than any other entertainers or groups.

2006 The NFL Cheerleader Playoffs air on television. Cheerleaders from 25 NFL teams compete. They do athletic events and trivia. They perform dances. Cheerleaders from the San Diego Chargers win.

2019 Male cheerleaders perform at the Super Bowl for the first time. They are part of the Los Angeles Rams' sideline team.

Professional Cheerleading

Kansas City Chiefs cheerleaders arrive at the stadium four hours before games begin. First, they have a team meeting. Then, they practice routines on the field.

10　Cheerleading

How Professional Cheerleading Works

The sports leagues for which cheerleaders perform set the cheerleading rules. The NFL's minimum age for cheerleaders is 18. The NBA's is 21. The NFL requires its cheerleaders to have a high school diploma. Individual teams also have strict rules. Rules are set for attendance. Appearance and **etiquette** are also covered.

To form squads each year, professional teams host tryouts. The process can take several weeks. Hundreds of women try out. There are usually only two or three dozen spots per team. Most of the time, cheerleaders have other jobs. Many are students. Professional cheerleaders still work up to 40 hours per week. This includes practice and games. Cheerleaders also attend many special events.

Only **10 percent** of the **8,000 cheerleaders** who try out for the NFL each year get a spot on a team.

The Warrior Girls cheer for the NBA's Golden State Warriors. They practice twice a week and two hours before games.

Professional Cheerleading

Athletes and Coaches

Many people support the work of professional cheerleaders. A squad's coach is sometimes called a director. The director hires cheerleaders. He or she schedules practices. The director also makes sure members follow team rules. He or she creates and teaches routines.

Tracy Sormanti has been cheerleading director for the New England Patriots since 1994.

All cheerleaders must be strong and fit. Some teams hire athletic trainers. Athletic trainers lead workouts. They educate the cheerleaders about how to do difficult cheer moves safely and without injury.

The captain is the team's leader. Often, there are multiple captains. Each captain is in charge of one line of dancers. Captains can be selected in different ways, depending on the team. Sometimes, they are selected by the director. They might also **nominate** themselves.

During tryouts, squad captains teach routines to cheerleading hopefuls.

Professional Cheerleading

The Right Tools

Professional cheerleaders do not need very much equipment to succeed. Game-day outfits, pom-poms, and protective braces are some of their most important items.

Pom-poms Cheerleaders wave pom-poms to attract fans' attention. Pom-poms are usually sparkly and in the team's colors.

Team Uniform Cheerleaders all wear the same uniform. Uniforms are in their team colors. They are sometimes in the style of the sports team's name. For example, uniforms for the Raiders cheerleaders have pirate-like sleeves. Squads wear different uniforms for special routines and holidays.

Protective Braces

Wraps or braces are often used during practice sessions. These tools protect injured or strained body parts. They prevent further injury. Braces are often used on ankles and knees. They also work well on wrists and elbows.

Hair and Makeup Styling Tools

Each cheerleader does his or her own hair and makeup. Cheerleaders can show individual personalities through hair and makeup choices. Some teams have beauty guidelines. These help cheerleaders look like they are on the same team. Teams might require female cheerleaders to wear their hair down. They might wear a certain color of lipstick.

Professional Cheerleading

The Right Moves

Professional cheerleading routines use standard cheer motions. They also work in jazz and hip-hop dance moves. **Tumbling** is not required, although it is often featured in routines.

Punch During the classic punch move, one arm punches straight up. The other rests on the hip in a fist. The punch can be done on either side of the body.

T and Half T In a T, the cheerleader's arms are straight out. Hands are in fists. The shoulders are relaxed. In a Half T, the cheerleader's arms are bent at the elbow. Fists are held at the shoulders. The upper arms and forearms are pressed against each other. Pinkies are facing out, with thumbs facing the shoulders.

Ball, Change, Step The ball, change, step is a common dance move in many styles of dance, including hip-hop. It is also easily added to cheer routines. The move starts with the feet together. The right foot steps back behind the left foot. The ball of the right foot rests on the ground. The front leg steps to the right, while the right foot stays in position. The right foot steps forward and out. The move ends with the feet spread shoulder-width apart. The move is then repeated with the other foot.

Heel Stretch The heel stretch begins with one leg kicking up. The arm on the same side as that leg grabs the heel. The heel is pulled toward the face. The kicked leg and arm should be straight. The other arm is held up, with the hand in a fist.

Professional Cheerleading 17

Getting Involved

To be successful, professional cheerleaders have to be passionate performers. They also have to be skilled dancers. If you want to follow in their footsteps, there are actions you can take now.

1. Start by working on tumbling. Begin with basic moves. Try somersaults, jumps, and leaps.

Hip-hop dance started in U.S. cities. It is now taught at studios and gyms around the world.

2. You can also take dance classes. Focus on hip-hop and jazz dance. These dance styles are a large part of professional routines. Practice the dance moves from this book.

3. Learn more about the life of a professional cheerleader. You can find a squad close to home. Watch videos of the team's moves. Try to practice their routines.

4. See if there is a NBA or NFL team near you. Many teams have junior cheer squads. First, find out about their application rules and deadlines. Then, you can try to join. You can learn cheer moves and routines from the professionals. You might even get to cheer at a game.

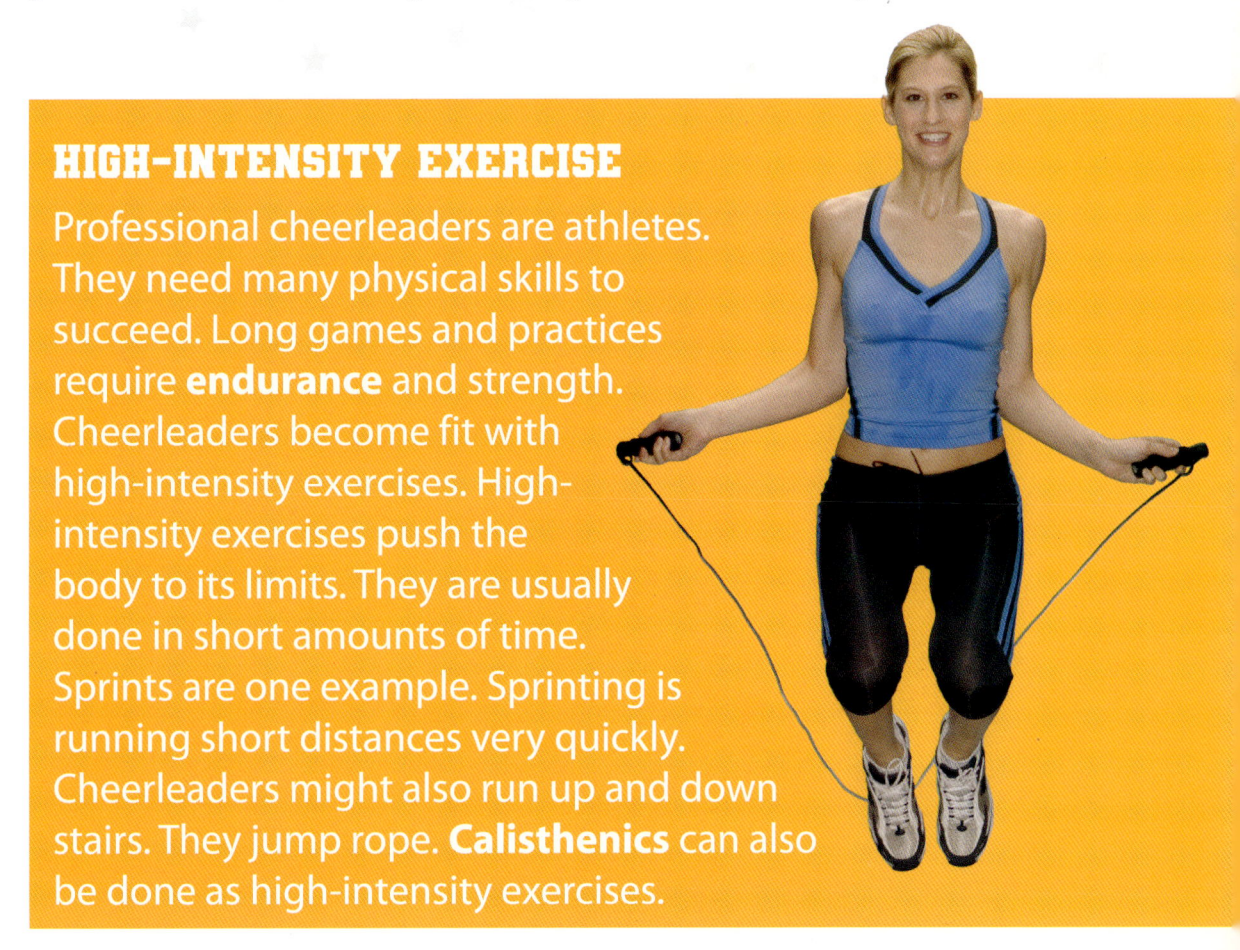

HIGH-INTENSITY EXERCISE

Professional cheerleaders are athletes. They need many physical skills to succeed. Long games and practices require **endurance** and strength. Cheerleaders become fit with high-intensity exercises. High-intensity exercises push the body to its limits. They are usually done in short amounts of time. Sprints are one example. Sprinting is running short distances very quickly. Cheerleaders might also run up and down stairs. They jump rope. **Calisthenics** can also be done as high-intensity exercises.

Professional Cheerleading   19

PROFILE

Regina Bailey

Science Cheerleader is a group with more than 300 members. All members are NFL or NBA cheerleaders. They also work in **STEM** fields. Science Cheerleader wants to inspire girls to enter these fields.

Regina Bailey was a cheerleader for the Washington Redskins. She is now part of Science Cheerleader. Bailey is an emergency room doctor. She teaches medicine, too. Bailey has a medical degree from George Washington University. She also has a degree in health law.

Bailey wants to change **stereotypes** about scientists. This is why she works with Science Cheerleader. Bailey wants to show that scientists can be people of all genders, races, and ages.

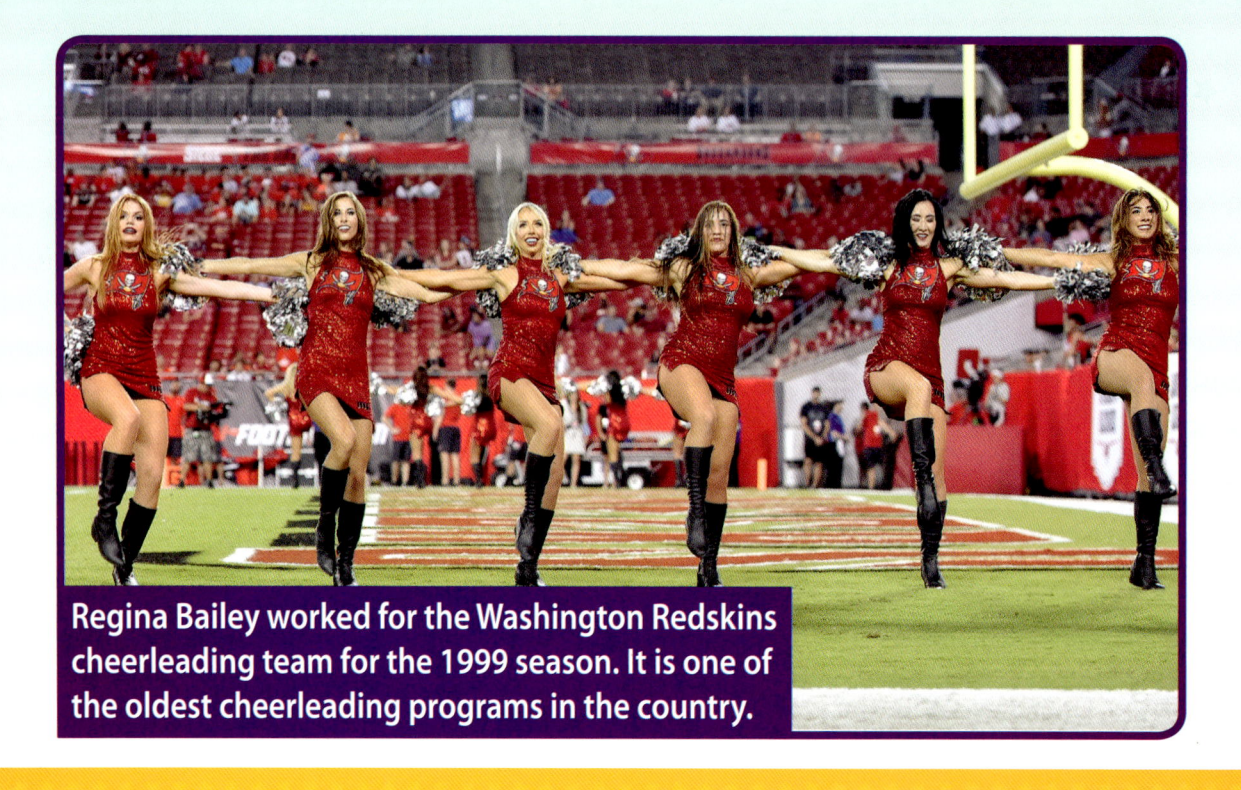

Regina Bailey worked for the Washington Redskins cheerleading team for the 1999 season. It is one of the oldest cheerleading programs in the country.

Members of Science Cheerleader tour the country. They give talks and work with young women.

Professional Cheerleading 21

Quiz

1 Which types of teams have professional cheerleaders?

Football and basketball

2 When did the New York Jets' Flight Team form?

2007

3 Which professional cheer team has performed the most USO shows?

The Dallas Cowboys Cheerleaders

4 What are the NFL and NBA minimum ages for cheerleaders?

18 and 21

5 Can there be more than one professional cheer team captain?

Yes

6 Why do professional cheerleaders use wraps and braces?

To protect body parts and prevent further injury

7 What are some examples of high-intensity exercises?

Sprints, stair running, jumping rope, and calisthenics

8 How many members does Science Cheerleader have?

More than 300

22 Cheerleading

Key Words

alumni: people who went to the same school or college

calisthenics: exercises that are done with just the body and without equipment, such as push-ups

charity: raising money or collecting items to help people in need

coeducational: including both males and females

endurance: an ability to keep going when tired or stressed

etiquette: ways to be polite and proper

nominate: to choose as a potential person to fill a position or job

publicity: appearances in the media, such as the news, movies, or internet

sideline: a type of cheerleading in which a team cheers on its sport team from the sides of the field

squad: a cheerleading team

STEM: having to do with science, technology, engineering, and mathematics

stereotypes: often untrue beliefs that people in certain groups are all the same

stunt: an advanced cheerleading move during which a cheerleader is held up or tossed in the air

tumbling: gymnastics moves, such as somersaults, rolls, and leaps

USO: stands for United Service Organizations, a program that provides support and entertainment to U.S. soldiers working around the world

Index

athletic trainers 13

Bailey, Regina 20

captain 13, 22

Dallas Cowboy Cheerleaders (DCC) 5, 6, 7, 8, 9, 22
director 12, 13

Indiana Pacemates 9

men in cheerleading 7, 9

National Basketball Association (NBA) 7, 9, 11, 19, 20, 22

National Football Cheerleaders Alumni Reunion 5

National Football League (NFL) 5, 7, 9, 11, 19, 20, 22

Raiderettes 4, 14

tryouts 7, 9, 11, 13

uniform 7, 8, 9, 14

Professional Cheerleading

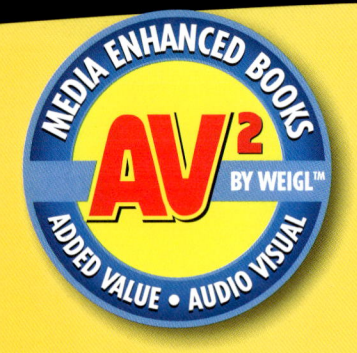

Log on to www.av2books.com

AV² by Weigl brings you media enhanced books that support active learning. Go to www.av2books.com, and enter the special code found on page 2 of this book. You will gain access to enriched and enhanced content that supplements and complements this book. Content includes video, audio, weblinks, quizzes, a slideshow, and activities.

AV² Online Navigation

Audio
Listen to sections of the book read aloud.

Book Pages
AV² pages directly correspond to pages in the book.

Video
Watch informative video clips.

Key Words
Study vocabulary, and complete a matching word activity.

Embedded Weblinks
Gain additional information for research.

Quizzes
Test your knowledge.

Slideshow
View images and captions, and prepare a presentation.

Try This!
Complete activities and hands-on experiments.

AV² was built to bridge the gap between print and digital. We encourage you to tell us what you like and what you want to see in the future.

Sign up to be an AV² Ambassador at www.av2books.com/ambassador.

Due to the dynamic nature of the internet, some of the URLs and activities provided as part of AV² by Weigl may have changed or ceased to exist. AV² by Weigl accepts no responsibility for any such changes. All media enhanced books are regularly monitored to update addresses and sites in a timely manner. Contact AV² by Weigl at 1-866-649-3445 or av2books@weigl.com with any questions, comments, or feedback.

24 Cheerleading